50 Brunch Buffet Recipes for Home

By: Kelly Johnson

Table of Contents

- Eggs Benedict
- Belgian Waffles
- Quiche Lorraine
- Blueberry Pancakes
- Breakfast Burritos
- French Toast Casserole
- Smoked Salmon Bagels
- Spinach and Feta Frittata
- Breakfast Hash
- Huevos Rancheros
- Avocado Toast with Poached Eggs
- Breakfast Tacos
- Sausage and Mushroom Strata
- Lemon Ricotta Pancakes
- Croque Monsieur
- Greek Yogurt Parfait
- Breakfast Pizza
- Shrimp and Grits
- Chilaquiles
- Cinnamon Roll French Toast Bake
- Breakfast Sliders
- Caprese Omelette
- Eggs Florentine
- Breakfast Quesadillas
- Banana Bread French Toast
- Asparagus and Goat Cheese Frittata
- Bacon and Egg Cups
- Cornbread Waffles
- Breakfast BLT Sandwiches
- Southwest Breakfast Skillet
- Biscuits and Gravy
- Smoked Salmon Quiche
- Zucchini and Tomato Frittata
- Breakfast Stromboli
- Breakfast Cobb Salad

- Monte Cristo Sandwiches
- Veggie Breakfast Burritos
- Breakfast Stuffed Peppers
- Hash Brown Casserole
- Brioche French Toast
- Chicken and Waffle Sliders
- Breakfast Empanadas
- Spinach and Bacon Quiche
- Caramelized Onion and Gruyere Quiche
- Breakfast Bruschetta
- Breakfast Enchiladas
- Breakfast Nachos
- Bacon and Cheddar Scones
- Ham and Cheese Croissants
- Breakfast Strata with Sausage and Peppers

Eggs Benedict

Ingredients:

- 4 English muffins, split and toasted
- 8 slices Canadian bacon or ham
- 8 large eggs
- Salt and pepper to taste
- Chopped fresh parsley or chives (optional), for garnish

For the Hollandaise Sauce:

- 3 large egg yolks
- 1 tablespoon water
- 1 tablespoon lemon juice
- 1/2 cup unsalted butter, melted
- Pinch of cayenne pepper
- Salt to taste

Instructions:

Prepare the Hollandaise sauce: In a heatproof bowl, whisk together the egg yolks, water, and lemon juice until well combined.
Place the bowl over a pot of simmering water (double boiler). Make sure the bottom of the bowl does not touch the water.
Whisk the egg mixture constantly while slowly drizzling in the melted butter.
Continue whisking until the sauce is thickened and smooth, about 3-5 minutes.
Season the Hollandaise sauce with cayenne pepper and salt to taste. Keep warm over low heat while you prepare the other components.
Poach the eggs: Fill a large saucepan with about 2 inches of water and bring it to a gentle simmer. Crack each egg into a small cup or ramekin.
Carefully slide each egg into the simmering water. Poach the eggs for about 3-4 minutes, until the whites are set but the yolks are still runny.
Using a slotted spoon, remove the poached eggs from the water and drain them on paper towels.
Assemble the Eggs Benedict: Place a slice of Canadian bacon or ham on each toasted English muffin half. Top each with a poached egg.
Spoon Hollandaise sauce generously over each poached egg.

Garnish with chopped parsley or chives, if desired. Serve immediately.

Enjoy your delicious Eggs Benedict!

Belgian Waffles

Ingredients:

- 2 cups all-purpose flour
- 2 tablespoons granulated sugar
- 1 tablespoon baking powder
- 1/2 teaspoon salt
- 2 large eggs, separated
- 1 3/4 cups milk
- 1/2 cup unsalted butter, melted
- 1 teaspoon vanilla extract

Instructions:

Preheat your Belgian waffle iron according to the manufacturer's instructions.
In a large mixing bowl, sift together the flour, sugar, baking powder, and salt.
In another bowl, whisk the egg yolks with the milk, melted butter, and vanilla extract until well combined.
Pour the wet ingredients into the dry ingredients and stir until just combined. Do not overmix; a few lumps are okay.
In a clean mixing bowl, beat the egg whites with a hand mixer or stand mixer until stiff peaks form.
Gently fold the beaten egg whites into the batter until just incorporated.
Lightly grease the waffle iron with cooking spray or brush with melted butter.
Pour enough batter onto the preheated waffle iron to cover the grids evenly. Close the lid and cook according to the manufacturer's instructions, or until the waffles are golden brown and crisp.
Carefully remove the waffles from the iron and serve immediately with your favorite toppings, such as maple syrup, fresh berries, whipped cream, or powdered sugar.
Repeat with the remaining batter, greasing the waffle iron as needed, until all the batter is used.
Enjoy your homemade Belgian waffles hot and fresh!

Feel free to add any variations or tips to this recipe to personalize it for your cookbook!

Quiche Lorraine

Ingredients:

- 1 pie crust (homemade or store-bought)
- 6 slices bacon, diced
- 1 small onion, finely chopped
- 1 cup shredded Gruyère cheese (or Swiss cheese)
- 4 large eggs
- 1 cup heavy cream
- 1/2 teaspoon salt
- 1/4 teaspoon black pepper
- Pinch of nutmeg (optional)
- Fresh parsley, chopped (for garnish)

Instructions:

Preheat your oven to 375°F (190°C). Place the pie crust in a 9-inch pie dish and crimp the edges. Prick the bottom of the crust with a fork and line it with parchment paper. Fill the crust with pie weights or dried beans to prevent it from puffing up during baking. Bake the crust for about 10 minutes, or until lightly golden. Remove from the oven and let cool slightly.
In a skillet, cook the diced bacon over medium heat until crispy. Remove the bacon from the skillet and drain on paper towels. Discard excess bacon fat, leaving about 1 tablespoon in the skillet.
In the same skillet with the reserved bacon fat, sauté the chopped onion over medium heat until softened and translucent, about 5 minutes. Remove from heat and let cool slightly.
Sprinkle the cooked bacon and sautéed onions evenly over the bottom of the partially baked pie crust. Sprinkle the shredded cheese on top.
In a mixing bowl, whisk together the eggs, heavy cream, salt, pepper, and nutmeg until well combined.
Pour the egg mixture over the bacon, onion, and cheese in the pie crust.
Place the quiche in the preheated oven and bake for 30-35 minutes, or until the filling is set and the top is golden brown.
Remove the quiche from the oven and let it cool for a few minutes before slicing. Garnish with chopped parsley before serving.
Enjoy your homemade Quiche Lorraine warm or at room temperature as a delicious breakfast, brunch, or light dinner option!

Feel free to adjust the ingredients or add any personal touches to customize the recipe to your taste preferences.

Blueberry Pancakes

Ingredients:

- 1 cup all-purpose flour
- 2 tablespoons granulated sugar
- 1 teaspoon baking powder
- 1/2 teaspoon baking soda
- 1/4 teaspoon salt
- 1 cup buttermilk
- 1 large egg
- 2 tablespoons unsalted butter, melted and cooled
- 1 teaspoon vanilla extract
- 1 cup fresh blueberries (or frozen, thawed)
- Butter or cooking spray for greasing the griddle
- Maple syrup, for serving

Instructions:

In a large mixing bowl, whisk together the flour, sugar, baking powder, baking soda, and salt.
In another bowl, whisk together the buttermilk, egg, melted butter, and vanilla extract until well combined.
Pour the wet ingredients into the dry ingredients and stir until just combined. Do not overmix; it's okay if there are some lumps in the batter.
Gently fold in the blueberries until evenly distributed throughout the batter.
Preheat a griddle or non-stick skillet over medium heat. Lightly grease the surface with butter or cooking spray.
Using a measuring cup or ladle, pour about 1/4 cup of batter onto the hot griddle for each pancake, spacing them apart to allow room for spreading.
Cook the pancakes for 2-3 minutes, or until bubbles form on the surface and the edges begin to look set.
Carefully flip the pancakes using a spatula and cook for an additional 1-2 minutes, or until golden brown and cooked through.
Transfer the cooked pancakes to a plate and keep warm while you cook the remaining batter. You may need to adjust the heat as you go to prevent burning.
Serve the blueberry pancakes warm with butter and maple syrup.

Enjoy your homemade blueberry pancakes as a delicious breakfast or brunch option!

Feel free to customize these pancakes by adding a sprinkle of cinnamon or lemon zest to the batter for extra flavor. You can also top them with additional fresh blueberries or a dollop of whipped cream for an extra special treat.

Breakfast Burritos

Ingredients:

- 6 large eggs
- 1/4 cup milk
- Salt and pepper, to taste
- 1 tablespoon unsalted butter or oil
- 4 large flour tortillas
- 1 cup shredded cheddar cheese
- 4 slices cooked bacon, chopped
- 1/2 cup diced cooked potatoes (such as hash browns or home fries)
- 1/4 cup diced bell peppers (optional)
- Salsa, avocado slices, sour cream, or hot sauce, for serving (optional)

Instructions:

In a mixing bowl, whisk together the eggs, milk, salt, and pepper until well combined.

In a large skillet, melt the butter over medium heat. Pour the beaten eggs into the skillet and cook, stirring occasionally, until scrambled and just set. Remove from heat.

Warm the flour tortillas in the microwave for a few seconds or in a dry skillet over medium heat for about 10-15 seconds per side to make them pliable.

Divide the scrambled eggs evenly among the tortillas, placing them in the center of each tortilla.

Sprinkle shredded cheddar cheese over the scrambled eggs on each tortilla.

Add chopped bacon, diced potatoes, and diced bell peppers (if using) evenly over the cheese layer.

Fold the sides of each tortilla over the filling, then fold the bottom edge up and roll tightly to form a burrito.

If desired, wrap each breakfast burrito in aluminum foil or parchment paper to keep them warm and secure while serving.

Serve the breakfast burritos with salsa, avocado slices, sour cream, or hot sauce on the side for dipping or topping, if desired.

Enjoy your homemade breakfast burritos as a satisfying and portable morning meal!

Feel free to customize these breakfast burritos by adding other ingredients such as cooked sausage, ham, mushrooms, onions, or spinach. You can also make a large batch and freeze them individually for quick and easy breakfasts on busy mornings.

French Toast Casserole

Ingredients:

- 1 loaf French bread (about 14-16 ounces), preferably a day old
- 8 large eggs
- 2 cups whole milk
- 1/2 cup heavy cream
- 1/4 cup granulated sugar
- 1/4 cup brown sugar
- 1 tablespoon vanilla extract
- 1 teaspoon ground cinnamon
- 1/4 teaspoon ground nutmeg
- Pinch of salt
- 1/2 cup chopped pecans or walnuts (optional)
- Maple syrup, for serving
- Powdered sugar, for dusting (optional)
- Fresh berries, for garnish (optional)

Instructions:

Grease a 9x13-inch baking dish with butter or cooking spray. Set aside.

Cut the French bread into cubes, about 1-inch in size. Spread the bread cubes evenly in the prepared baking dish.

In a large mixing bowl, whisk together the eggs, whole milk, heavy cream, granulated sugar, brown sugar, vanilla extract, cinnamon, nutmeg, and salt until well combined.

Pour the egg mixture evenly over the bread cubes in the baking dish, ensuring all the bread is coated. Gently press down on the bread with a spatula to help it absorb the liquid.

If using, sprinkle the chopped nuts over the top of the casserole.

Cover the baking dish with plastic wrap and refrigerate for at least 4 hours or overnight to allow the bread to soak up the egg mixture.

When ready to bake, preheat your oven to 350°F (175°C). Remove the plastic wrap from the baking dish.

Bake the French toast casserole in the preheated oven for 45-55 minutes, or until the top is golden brown and the center is set.

Remove the casserole from the oven and let it cool for a few minutes before serving.

Serve warm slices of French toast casserole with maple syrup drizzled over the top. Dust with powdered sugar and garnish with fresh berries, if desired.

Enjoy your homemade French toast casserole as a delicious and comforting breakfast treat!

Feel free to add other mix-ins such as chocolate chips, raisins, or sliced bananas for extra flavor and texture. You can also prepare the casserole the night before and bake it in the morning for a stress-free breakfast option.

Smoked Salmon Bagels

Ingredients:

- 4 bagels, sliced in half
- 8 ounces smoked salmon
- 4 ounces cream cheese, softened
- 1 tablespoon fresh dill, chopped
- 1 tablespoon capers, drained
- 1/4 red onion, thinly sliced
- 1 lemon, thinly sliced
- Freshly ground black pepper, to taste

Instructions:

Toast the bagel halves until lightly golden and crispy.
Spread a generous layer of cream cheese on each toasted bagel half.
Divide the smoked salmon evenly among the bagel halves, placing it on top of the cream cheese.
Sprinkle chopped fresh dill over the smoked salmon.
Scatter capers and thinly sliced red onion over the dill.
Place a couple of lemon slices on each bagel half.
Finish with a sprinkle of freshly ground black pepper, to taste.
Serve the smoked salmon bagels immediately as an open-faced sandwich.
Enjoy your homemade smoked salmon bagels as a delicious and satisfying breakfast or brunch option!

Feel free to customize these smoked salmon bagels by adding other toppings such as sliced cucumber, avocado, or tomato. You can also use flavored cream cheese or different types of bagels for variation.

Spinach and Feta Frittata

Ingredients:

- 8 large eggs
- 1/4 cup milk or heavy cream
- Salt and pepper, to taste
- 2 tablespoons olive oil
- 1 small onion, diced
- 2 cloves garlic, minced
- 4 cups fresh spinach leaves, chopped
- 1/2 cup crumbled feta cheese
- 2 tablespoons fresh parsley, chopped (optional, for garnish)

Instructions:

Preheat your oven to 350°F (175°C).
In a large mixing bowl, whisk together the eggs, milk or cream, salt, and pepper until well combined. Set aside.
In a 10-inch oven-safe skillet, heat the olive oil over medium heat. Add the diced onion and sauté until softened, about 3-4 minutes.
Add the minced garlic to the skillet and cook for another 1-2 minutes, until fragrant.
Add the chopped spinach to the skillet and cook, stirring occasionally, until wilted, about 2-3 minutes.
Spread the spinach mixture evenly in the skillet and pour the whisked egg mixture over the top.
Sprinkle the crumbled feta cheese evenly over the egg mixture.
Cook the frittata on the stovetop over medium heat for 3-4 minutes, or until the edges begin to set.
Transfer the skillet to the preheated oven and bake for 12-15 minutes, or until the frittata is set in the center and the top is lightly golden brown.
Remove the frittata from the oven and let it cool slightly in the skillet for a few minutes.
Use a spatula to loosen the edges of the frittata from the skillet, then slide it onto a serving plate.
Sprinkle chopped fresh parsley over the top for garnish, if desired.
Slice the frittata into wedges and serve warm.

Enjoy your homemade spinach and feta frittata as a delicious and satisfying meal!

Feel free to customize this frittata recipe by adding other ingredients such as diced bell peppers, mushrooms, or cooked bacon. You can also use different types of cheese according to your preference.

Breakfast Hash

Ingredients:

- 2 medium potatoes, diced into small cubes
- 1 small onion, diced
- 1 bell pepper, diced (optional)
- 2-3 slices of bacon or sausage, diced (optional)
- 2 tablespoons cooking oil or butter
- Salt and pepper to taste
- Optional seasonings: paprika, garlic powder, thyme, etc.
- Optional toppings: shredded cheese, chopped herbs, avocado slices, hot sauce, sour cream, etc.

Instructions:

Heat the cooking oil or melt the butter in a large skillet over medium heat.
Add the diced potatoes to the skillet and spread them out in a single layer. Cook, stirring occasionally, until the potatoes are golden brown and cooked through, about 10-15 minutes.
Once the potatoes are nearly cooked, add the diced onion and bell pepper to the skillet. Cook, stirring occasionally, until the vegetables are softened and slightly caramelized, about 5-7 minutes.
If using bacon or sausage, add it to the skillet with the vegetables and cook until crispy or cooked through, respectively.
Season the hash with salt, pepper, and any other desired seasonings, adjusting to taste.
Create wells in the hash for the eggs (if desired) and crack the eggs into the wells. Cover the skillet and cook until the eggs are cooked to your liking, either with runny yolks or fully set.
Once everything is cooked to your preference, remove the skillet from the heat. Serve the breakfast hash hot, optionally topped with shredded cheese, chopped herbs, avocado slices, hot sauce, sour cream, or any other desired toppings.

Enjoy your hearty and satisfying breakfast hash! Feel free to customize it with your favorite ingredients and flavors.

Huevos Rancheros

Ingredients:

- 4 corn tortillas
- 4 large eggs
- 1 cup refried beans (homemade or canned)
- 1 cup salsa (homemade or store-bought)
- 1/2 cup shredded cheese (such as cheddar or Monterey Jack)
- 1/4 cup chopped fresh cilantro (optional)
- Salt and pepper to taste
- Cooking oil

Instructions:

Warm the corn tortillas: You can do this by either heating them in a dry skillet over medium heat for about 30 seconds on each side or by wrapping them in a damp paper towel and microwaving them for about 30 seconds.
Heat the refried beans in a small saucepan over medium heat until heated through. Keep warm.
In another skillet, heat a small amount of cooking oil over medium heat. Once hot, crack the eggs into the skillet and cook them to your desired doneness, seasoning with salt and pepper to taste. You can cook them sunny-side up, over-easy, or however you prefer.
While the eggs are cooking, warm the salsa in a saucepan over medium heat until heated through.
Assemble the huevos rancheros: Place a warm corn tortilla on each plate. Spread a generous spoonful of refried beans onto each tortilla. Top with a fried egg.
Pour the warm salsa over the eggs and sprinkle with shredded cheese.
Garnish with chopped fresh cilantro, if desired.
Serve immediately, with additional salsa, hot sauce, or toppings of your choice on the side.

Enjoy your delicious huevos rancheros for a flavorful and satisfying breakfast!

Avocado Toast with Poached Eggs

Ingredients:

- 2 slices of bread (whole grain, sourdough, or your preferred choice)
- 1 ripe avocado
- 2 eggs
- 1 tablespoon white vinegar (for poaching eggs)
- Salt and pepper to taste
- Optional toppings: cherry tomatoes, feta cheese, red pepper flakes, microgreens, etc.

Instructions:

Toast the slices of bread to your desired level of crispiness.

While the bread is toasting, prepare the avocado. Cut the avocado in half, remove the pit, and scoop the flesh into a bowl. Mash the avocado with a fork until smooth, then season with salt and pepper to taste.

Once the toast is ready, spread the mashed avocado evenly onto each slice.

To poach the eggs, bring a medium-sized pot of water to a gentle simmer over medium heat. Add the white vinegar to the water.

Crack one egg into a small bowl or ramekin. Using a spoon, create a gentle whirlpool in the simmering water, then carefully slide the egg into the center of the whirlpool. Repeat with the second egg.

Cook the eggs in the simmering water for about 3-4 minutes for soft-poached eggs or longer if you prefer firmer yolks.

While the eggs are poaching, you can prepare any optional toppings you'd like to add to your avocado toast.

Once the eggs are cooked to your liking, use a slotted spoon to carefully remove them from the water and place them on top of the avocado toast.

Sprinkle additional salt and pepper on top of the poached eggs, and garnish with any optional toppings you desire.

Serve the avocado toast with poached eggs immediately while warm.

Enjoy your delicious and nutritious avocado toast with perfectly poached eggs! It's a simple yet satisfying meal that's packed with flavor and healthy fats.

Breakfast Tacos

Ingredients:

For the filling:

- 6 small corn or flour tortillas
- 6 large eggs
- 1 tablespoon olive oil or butter
- Salt and pepper to taste
- Optional fillings: cooked and crumbled bacon, cooked sausage, diced ham, black beans, sautéed vegetables (such as bell peppers, onions, and tomatoes), shredded cheese, avocado slices, salsa, hot sauce, chopped cilantro, diced jalapeños, etc.

Instructions:

Warm the tortillas: Heat a non-stick skillet over medium heat. Warm each tortilla for about 15-20 seconds on each side until they are soft and pliable. Stack them on a plate and cover with a clean kitchen towel to keep warm.
Prepare the filling: In the same skillet, heat olive oil or butter over medium heat. Crack the eggs into the skillet and season with salt and pepper. Cook, stirring gently, until the eggs are scrambled and just set, about 3-4 minutes. Remove from heat.
Assemble the tacos: Spoon some scrambled eggs onto each tortilla. Add your choice of optional fillings, such as cooked bacon, sausage, ham, black beans, sautéed vegetables, shredded cheese, avocado slices, salsa, hot sauce, chopped cilantro, or diced jalapeños.
Serve immediately: Fold the tortillas over the filling to form tacos and serve hot.
Enjoy your breakfast tacos: Customize them to your taste preferences and enjoy them as a hearty and delicious breakfast or brunch option!

Feel free to experiment with different fillings and toppings to create your favorite combination of breakfast tacos. They're versatile, easy to make, and sure to satisfy your morning cravings!

Sausage and Mushroom Strata

Ingredients:

- 8 slices of bread, preferably day-old and crusts removed
- 1 tablespoon olive oil
- 1/2 lb (225g) breakfast sausage, casings removed
- 1 cup sliced mushrooms
- 1 small onion, finely chopped
- 2 cloves garlic, minced
- 1 cup shredded cheese (such as cheddar, Swiss, or Monterey Jack)
- 6 large eggs
- 2 cups milk
- 1 teaspoon Dijon mustard
- 1/2 teaspoon salt
- 1/4 teaspoon black pepper
- Fresh herbs for garnish (optional)

Instructions:

Grease a 9x13 inch baking dish with butter or cooking spray. Arrange the bread slices in a single layer in the bottom of the dish, slightly overlapping if necessary. In a large skillet, heat the olive oil over medium heat. Add the breakfast sausage, breaking it up with a spoon, and cook until browned and cooked through, about 5-7 minutes.
Add the sliced mushrooms, chopped onion, and minced garlic to the skillet with the sausage. Cook, stirring occasionally, until the mushrooms are tender and the onions are translucent, about 5 minutes. Remove from heat and let cool slightly.
In a large mixing bowl, whisk together the eggs, milk, Dijon mustard, salt, and black pepper until well combined.
Sprinkle half of the shredded cheese over the bread slices in the baking dish. Top with the sausage and mushroom mixture, spreading it out evenly. Sprinkle the remaining cheese on top.
Pour the egg mixture evenly over the casserole, making sure to coat all the ingredients.
Cover the baking dish with plastic wrap and refrigerate for at least 4 hours or overnight, allowing the bread to absorb the egg mixture.

When ready to bake, preheat the oven to 350°F (175°C). Remove the plastic wrap from the baking dish and bake the strata in the preheated oven for 45-50 minutes, or until the top is golden brown and the center is set.
Let the strata cool for a few minutes before slicing. Garnish with fresh herbs if desired, then serve hot.

Enjoy your delicious sausage and mushroom strata as a hearty breakfast or brunch option! Leftovers can be refrigerated and reheated for later enjoyment.

Lemon Ricotta Pancakes

Ingredients:

- 1 cup all-purpose flour
- 1 tablespoon granulated sugar
- 1 teaspoon baking powder
- 1/2 teaspoon baking soda
- 1/4 teaspoon salt
- 1/2 cup ricotta cheese
- 3/4 cup milk
- 2 large eggs, separated
- Zest of 1 lemon
- 2 tablespoons freshly squeezed lemon juice
- 1 teaspoon vanilla extract
- Butter or oil for cooking
- Maple syrup and fresh berries for serving (optional)

Instructions:

In a large mixing bowl, whisk together the flour, sugar, baking powder, baking soda, and salt.

In another bowl, whisk together the ricotta cheese, milk, egg yolks, lemon zest, lemon juice, and vanilla extract until well combined.

Pour the wet ingredients into the dry ingredients and stir until just combined. Be careful not to overmix; a few lumps are okay.

In a clean mixing bowl, beat the egg whites with a hand mixer or stand mixer until stiff peaks form.

Gently fold the beaten egg whites into the pancake batter until just incorporated. This will help make the pancakes extra fluffy.

Heat a griddle or non-stick skillet over medium heat. Add a small amount of butter or oil to grease the surface.

Pour about 1/4 cup of batter onto the griddle for each pancake. Cook until bubbles form on the surface and the edges look set, about 2-3 minutes.

Carefully flip the pancakes and cook for an additional 1-2 minutes, or until golden brown and cooked through.

Transfer the cooked pancakes to a plate and keep warm while you cook the remaining batter. You may need to adjust the heat slightly as you cook to prevent burning.

Serve the lemon ricotta pancakes warm with maple syrup and fresh berries, if desired.

Enjoy your fluffy and flavorful lemon ricotta pancakes for a delightful breakfast or brunch treat! They're sure to be a hit with family and friends.

Croque Monsieur

Ingredients:

- Slices of good-quality bread (such as French bread or sourdough)
- Sliced ham (traditionally French ham like jambon de Paris)
- Gruyère cheese, grated (Emmental or Swiss cheese can also be used)
- Dijon mustard (optional)
- Butter
- Milk
- Flour
- Nutmeg (optional)
- Salt and pepper

Instructions:

Preheat your oven to around 375°F (190°C).
Start by making a béchamel sauce: In a small saucepan, melt a couple of tablespoons of butter over medium heat. Once melted, add an equal amount of flour to make a roux. Cook the roux for a minute or two until it's light golden brown and has a nutty aroma. Gradually whisk in milk, stirring constantly to avoid lumps. Cook until the sauce thickens, then season with salt, pepper, and a pinch of nutmeg if desired. Set aside.
If you're using Dijon mustard, spread a thin layer onto one side of each slice of bread.
Place slices of ham on half of the bread slices.
Sprinkle grated cheese generously over the ham.
Top with the remaining bread slices to form sandwiches.
Generously spread the béchamel sauce over the top of each sandwich. Make sure it covers the entire surface.
Sprinkle some more grated cheese on top of the béchamel sauce.
Arrange the sandwiches on a baking sheet and place in the preheated oven.
Bake for about 15-20 minutes, or until the sandwiches are heated through and the cheese is melted and bubbly. You can also broil briefly to get a golden crust on top if desired.
Once done, remove from the oven and let them cool for a couple of minutes before serving.

Croque Monsieur is often served with a simple green salad on the side. It's a delicious and satisfying dish, perfect for brunch, lunch, or a light dinner.

Greek Yogurt Parfait

Ingredients:

- Greek yogurt (plain or flavored, depending on your preference)
- Fresh fruits (such as berries, sliced bananas, diced mangoes, or any other fruits you like)
- Granola (homemade or store-bought)
- Honey, maple syrup, or agave nectar (optional, for added sweetness)
- Nuts or seeds (such as almonds, walnuts, or chia seeds) (optional, for extra crunch and nutrition)

Instructions:

Start by choosing your serving glasses or bowls. Parfaits are often served in clear glasses or jars to showcase the layers.

Begin by spooning a layer of Greek yogurt into the bottom of each glass. You can use plain Greek yogurt or flavored varieties like vanilla or honey.

Add a layer of fresh fruit on top of the yogurt. You can use a single type of fruit or mix different fruits together for variety and color.

Sprinkle a layer of granola over the fruit. Granola adds crunch and texture to the parfait and also provides additional fiber and nutrients.

If desired, drizzle a little honey, maple syrup, or agave nectar over the granola for added sweetness. This step is optional, especially if you're using flavored yogurt or very ripe and sweet fruits.

Repeat the layers until you reach the top of the glass, finishing with a final layer of Greek yogurt.

Garnish the top of the parfait with a few pieces of fresh fruit and a sprinkle of nuts or seeds for extra flavor and texture.

Serve immediately and enjoy your delicious and healthy Greek yogurt parfait!

Greek yogurt parfaits are versatile, and you can customize them according to your taste preferences and dietary needs. You can also make them ahead of time and store them in the refrigerator for a quick and convenient breakfast or snack option.

Breakfast Pizza

Ingredients:

For the pizza dough:

- 1 pound (about 450g) pizza dough, homemade or store-bought
- Cornmeal or flour, for dusting

For the toppings:

- 6 slices of bacon, cooked until crispy and chopped into pieces
- 4 large eggs
- Salt and pepper, to taste
- 1 cup shredded cheese (cheddar, mozzarella, or a blend)
- 1/2 cup diced bell peppers (red, green, or yellow)
- 1/4 cup diced red onion
- Fresh herbs such as parsley or chives, chopped (optional, for garnish)

Instructions:

Preheat your oven to the temperature recommended for your pizza dough (usually around 450°F or 230°C). If you're using a pizza stone, place it in the oven to preheat as well.

Roll out the pizza dough on a lightly floured surface or parchment paper to your desired thickness. Transfer the rolled-out dough to a baking sheet or pizza peel dusted with cornmeal or flour.

In a small bowl, beat the eggs with a pinch of salt and pepper.

Spread a thin layer of shredded cheese evenly over the pizza dough, leaving a border around the edges for the crust.

Sprinkle the chopped bacon over the cheese.

Scatter the diced bell peppers and red onion over the bacon.

Carefully pour the beaten eggs over the pizza, distributing them evenly.

Transfer the pizza to the preheated oven and bake for 12-15 minutes, or until the crust is golden brown and the eggs are set.

Once the pizza is done, remove it from the oven and let it cool for a few minutes.

Garnish the pizza with chopped fresh herbs, if desired.

Slice the breakfast pizza into wedges and serve hot.

Feel free to customize your breakfast pizza with additional toppings such as cooked sausage, ham, tomatoes, spinach, or mushrooms. Serve with a side of hot sauce or salsa for extra flavor, if desired. Enjoy your delicious homemade breakfast pizza!

Shrimp and Grits

Ingredients:

For the grits:

- 1 cup stone-ground grits
- 4 cups water or chicken broth
- Salt and pepper, to taste
- Butter or cheese (optional)

For the shrimp:

- 1 pound (about 450g) large shrimp, peeled and deveined
- Salt and pepper, to taste
- 2 tablespoons olive oil or butter
- 4 cloves garlic, minced
- 1 small onion, finely chopped
- 1 bell pepper, diced
- 1 cup diced tomatoes (fresh or canned)
- 1/2 cup chicken broth or white wine
- 1 teaspoon Cajun seasoning (or a mixture of paprika, garlic powder, onion powder, cayenne pepper, and thyme)
- Fresh parsley or green onions, chopped, for garnish

Instructions:

Start by preparing the grits. In a medium saucepan, bring the water or chicken broth to a boil. Stir in the grits and reduce the heat to low. Cook the grits, stirring occasionally, until thickened and creamy, about 20-25 minutes. Season with salt and pepper to taste. If desired, stir in butter or cheese for added richness.
While the grits are cooking, season the shrimp with salt and pepper.
In a large skillet, heat the olive oil or butter over medium-high heat. Add the minced garlic and sauté for about 1 minute, until fragrant.
Add the chopped onion and bell pepper to the skillet and cook until softened, about 5 minutes.
Stir in the diced tomatoes and cook for another 2-3 minutes.

Add the seasoned shrimp to the skillet and cook for 2-3 minutes per side, until they turn pink and opaque.

Pour in the chicken broth or white wine, and sprinkle the Cajun seasoning over the shrimp mixture. Stir to combine and let it simmer for a few minutes to allow the flavors to meld together.

Taste and adjust the seasoning with salt and pepper if needed.

To serve, spoon the creamy grits onto plates or bowls and top with the shrimp mixture.

Garnish with chopped parsley or green onions, and serve hot.

Enjoy your delicious homemade shrimp and grits as a comforting and flavorful meal!

Feel free to customize the dish by adding other ingredients such as bacon, sausage, or additional vegetables according to your taste preferences.

Chilaquiles

Ingredients:

For the salsa:

- 4 large tomatoes, quartered
- 1 onion, quartered
- 2 cloves garlic, peeled
- 1-2 jalapeño peppers (adjust to taste), stemmed and seeded
- Salt and pepper, to taste
- Handful of fresh cilantro leaves

For the chilaquiles:

- 10-12 corn tortillas, cut into triangles or strips
- Vegetable oil, for frying
- 1 cup shredded chicken, cooked (optional)
- 1 cup crumbled queso fresco or shredded cheese (such as Monterey Jack or cheddar)
- Crema or sour cream, for garnish
- Sliced avocado, for garnish
- Fresh cilantro leaves, for garnish
- Lime wedges, for serving

Instructions:

Start by making the salsa. In a blender or food processor, combine the quartered tomatoes, onion, garlic, jalapeño peppers, salt, pepper, and cilantro leaves. Blend until smooth. If the salsa is too thick, you can add a little water to achieve your desired consistency.

Heat about 1/2 inch of vegetable oil in a large skillet over medium-high heat. Once the oil is hot, fry the tortilla strips in batches until golden and crisp, about 2-3 minutes per batch. Use a slotted spoon to transfer the fried tortillas to a paper towel-lined plate to drain excess oil.

In the same skillet, pour the salsa and bring it to a simmer over medium heat. Let it cook for about 5 minutes to allow the flavors to meld together.

Add the fried tortilla strips to the simmering salsa, stirring gently to coat them evenly. If using shredded chicken, add it to the skillet and stir to combine.

Let the chilaquiles simmer for a few minutes, until the tortilla strips soften slightly but are still holding their shape.

Remove the skillet from the heat and sprinkle the crumbled queso fresco or shredded cheese over the top of the chilaquiles.

To serve, garnish the chilaquiles with dollops of crema or sour cream, sliced avocado, and fresh cilantro leaves. Serve with lime wedges on the side for squeezing over the dish.

Enjoy your delicious homemade chilaquiles as a hearty and flavorful breakfast or brunch option!

Chilaquiles can also be served with fried or scrambled eggs on top for added protein and richness, or alongside refried beans for a complete meal. Feel free to adjust the level of spiciness in the salsa to suit your taste preferences.

Cinnamon Roll French Toast Bake

Ingredients:

For the cinnamon roll layer:

- 1 tube (8-count) refrigerated cinnamon rolls with icing (such as Pillsbury Grands! Cinnamon Rolls)

For the French toast layer:

- 8 large eggs
- 1 cup milk (whole milk or any milk of your choice)
- 1 teaspoon vanilla extract
- 1/2 teaspoon ground cinnamon
- Pinch of salt

For the topping:

- Icing from the cinnamon roll tube (included in the package)
- Maple syrup, for serving
- Powdered sugar, for dusting (optional)

Instructions:

Preheat your oven to 350°F (175°C). Grease a 9x13-inch baking dish with butter or cooking spray.

Cut each cinnamon roll into quarters and spread them evenly in the prepared baking dish.

In a large mixing bowl, whisk together the eggs, milk, vanilla extract, ground cinnamon, and salt until well combined.

Pour the egg mixture evenly over the cinnamon roll pieces in the baking dish, making sure to coat them completely.

Cover the baking dish with aluminum foil and refrigerate for at least 1 hour or overnight. This allows the cinnamon rolls to absorb the egg mixture and develop flavor.

When ready to bake, preheat your oven to 350°F (175°C). Remove the baking dish from the refrigerator and let it sit at room temperature while the oven preheats.

Once the oven is preheated, bake the French toast casserole, covered with foil, for 25-30 minutes.

After 25-30 minutes, remove the foil and continue baking for an additional 10-15 minutes, or until the French toast is golden brown and cooked through.

Once done, remove the baking dish from the oven and let it cool for a few minutes.

Drizzle the icing from the cinnamon roll tube over the top of the French toast bake.
Serve warm with maple syrup and a dusting of powdered sugar, if desired.
Enjoy your delicious Cinnamon Roll French Toast Bake as a special treat for breakfast or brunch!

This dish can be customized by adding chopped nuts or raisins to the cinnamon roll layer or by incorporating a cream cheese drizzle instead of the icing for an extra indulgent touch.

Breakfast Sliders

Ingredients:

- 12 slider buns (such as Hawaiian rolls)
- 6 large eggs
- 6 slices of bacon, cooked until crispy
- 6 slices of cheese (such as cheddar, Swiss, or American)
- Salt and pepper, to taste
- Butter, for greasing the baking dish
- Optional toppings: sliced avocado, tomato slices, spinach leaves, hot sauce, mayonnaise

Instructions:

Preheat your oven to 350°F (175°C). Grease a baking dish large enough to fit all the slider buns.
In a large skillet, cook the bacon until crispy. Remove the bacon from the skillet and drain on paper towels. Once cooled, break each slice of bacon in half so that you have 12 pieces in total.
In the same skillet, crack the eggs and scramble them over medium heat. Season with salt and pepper to taste. Cook the scrambled eggs until they are just set but still moist. Remove from heat.
Slice the slider buns in half horizontally, keeping them attached as a single sheet. Place the bottom half of the slider buns in the greased baking dish.
Layer the scrambled eggs evenly over the bottom half of the slider buns.
Place a slice of cheese on top of the scrambled eggs.
Arrange the bacon pieces on top of the cheese.
Place the top half of the slider buns over the bacon to form sandwiches.
Cover the baking dish with aluminum foil and bake in the preheated oven for about 10-15 minutes, or until the cheese is melted and the sliders are heated through.
Remove the foil and bake for an additional 2-3 minutes to lightly toast the tops of the buns.
Once done, remove the breakfast sliders from the oven and let them cool slightly. Use a knife to cut the sliders into individual portions.
Serve warm and enjoy! Optionally, you can add toppings such as sliced avocado, tomato slices, spinach leaves, hot sauce, or mayonnaise to customize your breakfast sliders according to your taste preferences.

These breakfast sliders are versatile, and you can customize them with your favorite breakfast ingredients such as sausage, ham, or different types of cheese. They're perfect for brunch gatherings, potlucks, or meal prep for busy mornings.

Caprese Omelette

Ingredients:

- 3 large eggs
- 1 medium tomato, sliced
- 2-3 ounces fresh mozzarella cheese, sliced or diced
- Fresh basil leaves, torn or chopped
- Salt and pepper, to taste
- Olive oil or butter, for cooking
- Balsamic glaze or reduction (optional, for serving)

Instructions:

Crack the eggs into a mixing bowl and whisk them together until well combined. Season with salt and pepper to taste.
Heat a non-stick skillet over medium heat and add a small amount of olive oil or butter to coat the bottom of the pan.
Once the skillet is hot, pour the whisked eggs into the pan, tilting it to spread the eggs evenly.
Allow the eggs to cook undisturbed for a minute or two, until the edges start to set.
Using a spatula, gently lift the edges of the omelette and tilt the pan to let the uncooked eggs flow to the edges.
When the omelette is mostly set but still slightly runny on top, arrange the sliced tomatoes, mozzarella cheese, and torn basil leaves on one half of the omelette.
Carefully fold the other half of the omelette over the filling, creating a semi-circle shape.
Cook the omelette for another minute or two, until the cheese is melted and the filling is heated through.
Slide the omelette onto a plate and garnish with additional fresh basil leaves if desired.
If using, drizzle balsamic glaze or reduction over the top of the omelette for extra flavor.
Serve the Caprese omelette hot and enjoy!

This omelette makes for a delicious and satisfying breakfast or brunch option. You can also customize it by adding other ingredients such as cooked bacon, spinach, or mushrooms, according to your taste preferences.

Eggs Florentine

Ingredients:

- 2 English muffins, split and toasted
- 4 large eggs
- 2 cups fresh spinach, washed and chopped
- 1 tablespoon butter
- Salt and pepper to taste
- Hollandaise sauce (store-bought or homemade)

Instructions:

Prepare the hollandaise sauce if you're making it from scratch or warm up the store-bought one according to the package instructions. Keep it warm until ready to serve.

In a skillet, melt the butter over medium heat. Add the chopped spinach and cook until wilted, about 2-3 minutes. Season with salt and pepper to taste. Remove from heat and set aside.

To poach the eggs, bring a large pot of water to a gentle simmer. Crack each egg into a small bowl or cup. Using a spoon, create a gentle whirlpool in the water, then carefully slide each egg into the center of the whirlpool. Poach the eggs for about 3-4 minutes for runny yolks or longer if you prefer firmer yolks.

While the eggs are poaching, assemble the dish. Place the toasted English muffin halves on plates. Divide the cooked spinach evenly among the muffin halves, spreading it out into a layer.

Once the eggs are poached to your desired doneness, carefully remove them from the water with a slotted spoon and place them on top of the spinach.

Spoon hollandaise sauce generously over each egg.

Garnish with a sprinkle of freshly ground black pepper or chopped parsley if desired.

Serve immediately and enjoy your delicious Eggs Florentine!

Feel free to customize this recipe by adding extras like smoked salmon or avocado slices, or by substituting the English muffins with other bread like toasted sourdough or bagels.

Breakfast Quesadillas

Ingredients:

- 4 large flour tortillas
- 4 large eggs
- 1 cup shredded cheese (cheddar, Monterey Jack, or a Mexican cheese blend)
- 4 slices of cooked bacon or sausage, chopped (optional)
- 1/2 cup diced bell peppers (any color)
- 1/4 cup diced onions
- Salt and pepper to taste
- Cooking oil or butter for frying

Optional toppings:

- Salsa
- Sour cream
- Avocado slices
- Chopped cilantro

Instructions:

In a bowl, whisk the eggs and season with salt and pepper to taste.
Heat a non-stick skillet over medium heat and add a little oil or butter.
Pour the beaten eggs into the skillet and scramble until cooked through. Remove from the skillet and set aside.
In the same skillet, add a little more oil or butter if needed and sauté the diced bell peppers and onions until they are tender. Remove from the skillet and set aside.
Wipe the skillet clean with a paper towel and return it to the stove over medium heat.
Place one tortilla in the skillet and sprinkle a layer of shredded cheese evenly over the entire tortilla.
Spoon some scrambled eggs, cooked bacon or sausage (if using), and sautéed bell peppers and onions over half of the tortilla.
Fold the tortilla in half to cover the filling, pressing down gently with a spatula.
Cook the quesadilla for 2-3 minutes on each side, or until the tortilla is golden brown and crispy, and the cheese is melted.
Repeat the process with the remaining tortillas and filling ingredients.

Once all the quesadillas are cooked, remove them from the skillet and let them cool for a minute or two before cutting them into wedges.

Serve the breakfast quesadillas hot with your favorite toppings such as salsa, sour cream, avocado slices, or chopped cilantro.

Feel free to customize the filling with ingredients like cooked ham, diced tomatoes, black beans, or jalapeños to suit your taste preferences. Enjoy your delicious breakfast quesadillas!

Banana Bread French Toast

Ingredients:

- 4 thick slices of banana bread (homemade or store-bought)
- 2 large eggs
- 1/2 cup milk (whole milk or any milk of your choice)
- 1 teaspoon vanilla extract
- 1/2 teaspoon ground cinnamon
- Butter or cooking spray for greasing the skillet
- Maple syrup, sliced bananas, chopped nuts, or whipped cream for serving (optional)

Instructions:

In a shallow dish or bowl, whisk together the eggs, milk, vanilla extract, and ground cinnamon until well combined. This will be your French toast batter.
Preheat a skillet or griddle over medium heat. Add a small amount of butter or coat with cooking spray to prevent sticking.
Dip each slice of banana bread into the egg mixture, ensuring both sides are well coated. Allow any excess batter to drip off.
Place the dipped banana bread slices onto the preheated skillet or griddle. Cook for 2-3 minutes on each side, or until golden brown and cooked through.
Once cooked, transfer the banana bread French toast slices to a serving plate.
Serve the banana bread French toast hot with your favorite toppings, such as maple syrup, sliced bananas, chopped nuts, or whipped cream.
Enjoy your delicious and indulgent banana bread French toast!

Feel free to experiment with the toppings or add-ins. You can also sprinkle a little powdered sugar over the top for an extra touch of sweetness. This recipe is perfect for a special breakfast or brunch treat!

Asparagus and Goat Cheese Frittata

Ingredients:

- 8 large eggs
- 1/4 cup milk or heavy cream
- Salt and pepper to taste
- 1 tablespoon olive oil
- 1 bunch asparagus, tough ends trimmed, and cut into 1-inch pieces
- 1 small onion, diced
- 2 cloves garlic, minced
- 4 ounces goat cheese, crumbled
- 2 tablespoons chopped fresh herbs (such as parsley, chives, or basil)

Instructions:

Preheat your oven to 375°F (190°C).
In a large mixing bowl, whisk together the eggs, milk or heavy cream, salt, and pepper until well combined. Set aside.
Heat olive oil in a large oven-safe skillet over medium heat. Add the diced onion and cook until softened, about 3-4 minutes.
Add the minced garlic to the skillet and cook for an additional 1 minute, or until fragrant.
Add the asparagus pieces to the skillet and cook for 5-6 minutes, or until they are bright green and slightly tender.
Spread the asparagus and onion mixture evenly across the skillet. Pour the egg mixture over the vegetables, making sure they are evenly distributed.
Sprinkle the crumbled goat cheese evenly over the top of the frittata mixture.
Cook the frittata on the stovetop for 3-4 minutes, or until the edges start to set.
Transfer the skillet to the preheated oven and bake for 12-15 minutes, or until the frittata is set in the center and lightly golden brown on top.
Once cooked, remove the skillet from the oven and let the frittata cool for a few minutes.
Sprinkle the chopped fresh herbs over the top of the frittata.
Slice the frittata into wedges and serve warm or at room temperature.

Enjoy your delicious asparagus and goat cheese frittata as a satisfying and flavorful meal! You can also serve it with a side salad or some crusty bread for a complete meal.

Bacon and Egg Cups

Ingredients:

- 6 slices of bacon
- 6 large eggs
- Salt and pepper to taste
- Chopped fresh herbs (optional, for garnish)

Instructions:

Preheat your oven to 375°F (190°C). Lightly grease a 6-cup muffin tin with cooking spray or butter.

Take each slice of bacon and line the sides of each muffin cup, creating a circle. The bacon should come up to the top edge of the cup. You can also crisscross two slices of bacon to create a basket-like effect.

Crack one egg into each bacon-lined muffin cup. Season each egg with a pinch of salt and pepper.

Place the muffin tin in the preheated oven and bake for 15-20 minutes, or until the egg whites are set and the yolks are cooked to your desired doneness. Keep an eye on them towards the end of the cooking time to avoid overcooking the yolks.

Once cooked, remove the bacon and egg cups from the oven. Use a butter knife or offset spatula to gently loosen the edges of the cups if needed.

Carefully transfer the bacon and egg cups to a serving platter. Sprinkle with chopped fresh herbs like parsley or chives, if desired, for garnish.

Serve the bacon and egg cups hot, either on their own or with toast, avocado slices, or a side of fresh fruit.

These bacon and egg cups are not only delicious but also customizable. You can add shredded cheese, diced vegetables, or even cooked sausage to the cups before cracking the eggs for extra flavor. Enjoy your tasty breakfast treat!

Cornbread Waffles

Ingredients:

- 1 cup all-purpose flour
- 1 cup cornmeal
- 2 tablespoons granulated sugar
- 1 tablespoon baking powder
- 1/2 teaspoon baking soda
- 1/2 teaspoon salt
- 1 1/4 cups buttermilk
- 2 large eggs
- 1/4 cup unsalted butter, melted
- Cooking spray or additional butter for greasing the waffle iron

Instructions:

Preheat your waffle iron according to the manufacturer's instructions.
In a large mixing bowl, whisk together the all-purpose flour, cornmeal, granulated sugar, baking powder, baking soda, and salt until well combined.
In a separate bowl, whisk together the buttermilk, eggs, and melted butter until smooth.
Pour the wet ingredients into the dry ingredients and stir until just combined. Be careful not to overmix; a few lumps are okay.
Lightly grease the waffle iron with cooking spray or brush with melted butter.
Pour enough batter onto the preheated waffle iron to cover the waffle grid. The amount of batter will depend on the size of your waffle iron.
Close the waffle iron and cook the waffles according to the manufacturer's instructions, or until they are golden brown and crispy.
Carefully remove the cornbread waffles from the waffle iron and transfer them to a serving plate.
Repeat the process with the remaining batter, greasing the waffle iron as needed.
Serve the cornbread waffles hot with your favorite toppings, such as butter and maple syrup, honey, jam, or whipped cream.

These cornbread waffles are delicious on their own or paired with savory toppings like fried chicken or chili for a unique and satisfying meal. Enjoy!

Breakfast BLT Sandwiches

Ingredients:

- 8 slices of bacon
- 4 large eggs
- 4 slices of bread (white, whole wheat, or your preferred type)
- 4 leaves of lettuce
- 1 large tomato, sliced
- Mayonnaise
- Salt and pepper to taste

Instructions:

Cook the bacon in a skillet over medium heat until crispy, about 8-10 minutes. Remove the bacon from the skillet and place it on paper towels to drain excess grease. Keep warm.
While the bacon is cooking, toast the bread slices in a toaster or on a skillet until golden brown.
In the same skillet used to cook the bacon, fry the eggs to your desired doneness (sunny-side-up, over-easy, or scrambled). Season the eggs with salt and pepper to taste.
To assemble each sandwich, spread a thin layer of mayonnaise on one side of each toasted bread slice.
Place a leaf of lettuce on one slice of bread.
Top the lettuce with 2 slices of tomato.
Place 2 slices of cooked bacon on top of the tomato.
Carefully place a cooked egg on top of the bacon.
Place the second slice of bread on top of the egg, mayo-side down, to complete the sandwich.
Repeat the process to assemble the remaining sandwiches.
If desired, you can slice the sandwiches in half diagonally before serving.
Serve the breakfast BLT sandwiches immediately while still warm and enjoy!

Feel free to customize your breakfast BLT sandwiches by adding avocado slices, cheese, or your favorite condiments. They're versatile and sure to be a hit at the breakfast table!

Southwest Breakfast Skillet

Ingredients:

- 4 medium potatoes, diced into small cubes
- 1 tablespoon olive oil
- 1 small onion, diced
- 1 bell pepper (any color), diced
- 2 cloves garlic, minced
- 1 teaspoon ground cumin
- 1 teaspoon chili powder
- Salt and pepper to taste
- 4 large eggs
- 1 cup shredded cheese (cheddar, Monterey Jack, or a Mexican cheese blend)
- Optional toppings: salsa, avocado slices, chopped cilantro, sour cream

Instructions:

Heat the olive oil in a large skillet over medium heat. Add the diced potatoes and cook, stirring occasionally, until they are golden brown and crispy, about 10-12 minutes.

Add the diced onion and bell pepper to the skillet with the potatoes. Cook for an additional 5 minutes, or until the vegetables are softened.

Stir in the minced garlic, ground cumin, and chili powder. Cook for 1 minute, until fragrant.

Create 4 wells in the potato mixture with a spoon. Crack one egg into each well. Season the eggs with salt and pepper to taste.

Cover the skillet with a lid and cook for 5-7 minutes, or until the egg whites are set and the yolks are cooked to your desired doneness. If you prefer firmer yolks, cook them for a few minutes longer.

Sprinkle the shredded cheese evenly over the skillet. Cover again and cook for an additional 1-2 minutes, or until the cheese is melted.

Once the cheese is melted and the eggs are cooked to your liking, remove the skillet from the heat.

Serve the Southwest breakfast skillet hot, topped with your choice of optional toppings such as salsa, avocado slices, chopped cilantro, or sour cream.

Enjoy your flavorful and satisfying Southwest breakfast skillet!

Feel free to customize this recipe by adding cooked bacon, sausage, or black beans for extra protein and flavor. It's a versatile dish that's perfect for breakfast, brunch, or even dinner!

Biscuits and Gravy

Ingredients for Biscuits:

- 2 cups all-purpose flour
- 1 tablespoon baking powder
- 1 teaspoon salt
- 1/2 cup unsalted butter, cold and cut into small cubes
- 3/4 cup milk

Ingredients for Gravy:

- 1/2 pound breakfast sausage (pork or turkey)
- 2 tablespoons unsalted butter
- 1/4 cup all-purpose flour
- 2 cups milk
- Salt and pepper to taste

Instructions:

Preheat your oven to 425°F (220°C).
In a large mixing bowl, whisk together the flour, baking powder, and salt.
Add the cold cubed butter to the flour mixture. Using a pastry cutter or your fingertips, cut the butter into the flour until the mixture resembles coarse crumbs.
Pour the milk into the flour mixture and stir until just combined. Be careful not to overmix.
Turn the dough out onto a lightly floured surface and gently knead it a few times until it comes together. Pat the dough into a circle about 1 inch thick.
Use a biscuit cutter or a glass to cut out biscuits from the dough. Place the biscuits on a baking sheet lined with parchment paper, leaving a little space between each one.
Bake the biscuits in the preheated oven for 12-15 minutes, or until they are golden brown on top.
While the biscuits are baking, prepare the gravy. In a skillet, cook the breakfast sausage over medium heat, breaking it up into crumbles with a spatula, until it is browned and cooked through.
Once the sausage is cooked, add the butter to the skillet and let it melt.
Sprinkle the flour over the sausage and butter mixture, stirring constantly, and cook for 1-2 minutes to form a roux.

Slowly pour the milk into the skillet while stirring continuously to prevent lumps from forming.
Cook the gravy, stirring frequently, until it thickens to your desired consistency.
Season with salt and pepper to taste.
Once the biscuits are done baking, split them in half and place them on serving plates.
Spoon the sausage gravy over the biscuits.
Serve the biscuits and gravy hot, and enjoy this comforting and satisfying dish!

Feel free to adjust the seasoning and thickness of the gravy according to your taste preferences. You can also add a dash of hot sauce or Worcestershire sauce for extra flavor if desired.

Smoked Salmon Quiche

Ingredients:

For the crust:

- 1 1/4 cups all-purpose flour
- 1/2 teaspoon salt
- 1/2 cup (1 stick) unsalted butter, cold and cut into small cubes
- 2-4 tablespoons ice water

For the filling:

- 6 ounces smoked salmon, chopped or thinly sliced
- 1 cup shredded Swiss cheese (or any cheese of your choice)
- 4 large eggs
- 1 cup half-and-half (or whole milk)
- 1/4 cup chopped fresh dill
- 1/4 teaspoon salt
- 1/4 teaspoon black pepper
- 1/4 teaspoon paprika

Instructions:

Preheat your oven to 375°F (190°C).
To make the crust, in a food processor, combine the flour and salt. Add the cold cubed butter and pulse until the mixture resembles coarse crumbs.
Gradually add the ice water, 1 tablespoon at a time, and pulse until the dough comes together. Be careful not to overmix. You may not need to use all the water.
Turn the dough out onto a lightly floured surface and shape it into a disk. Wrap the dough in plastic wrap and refrigerate it for at least 30 minutes.
After chilling, roll out the dough on a floured surface into a circle large enough to fit into a 9-inch pie dish. Carefully transfer the dough to the pie dish and press it into the bottom and up the sides. Trim any excess dough and crimp the edges. Prick the bottom of the crust with a fork. Line the crust with parchment paper or aluminum foil and fill it with pie weights or dried beans.

Bake the crust in the preheated oven for 15 minutes. Remove the parchment paper and weights and bake for an additional 5 minutes, or until the crust is lightly golden brown. Remove from the oven and set aside.

Reduce the oven temperature to 350°F (175°C).

In a bowl, whisk together the eggs, half-and-half, chopped dill, salt, pepper, and paprika until well combined.

Sprinkle the chopped smoked salmon and shredded Swiss cheese evenly over the bottom of the pre-baked pie crust.

Pour the egg mixture over the smoked salmon and cheese in the pie crust.

Bake the quiche in the preheated oven for 35-40 minutes, or until the filling is set and the top is golden brown.

Remove the quiche from the oven and let it cool for a few minutes before slicing and serving.

Serve the smoked salmon quiche warm or at room temperature. Enjoy!

Feel free to customize this recipe by adding ingredients like caramelized onions, spinach, or roasted red peppers to the filling. It's a versatile dish that's sure to impress!

Zucchini and Tomato Frittata

Ingredients:

- 6 large eggs
- 1 medium zucchini, thinly sliced
- 1 large tomato, thinly sliced
- 1/2 cup shredded cheese (such as mozzarella, cheddar, or feta)
- 1/4 cup chopped fresh basil or parsley
- 2 tablespoons olive oil
- Salt and pepper to taste

Instructions:

> Preheat your oven to 350°F (175°C).
> In a large mixing bowl, beat the eggs until well combined. Season with salt and pepper to taste.
> Heat the olive oil in an oven-safe skillet (preferably non-stick) over medium heat.
> Add the sliced zucchini to the skillet and sauté for 3-4 minutes, or until slightly softened.
> Add the sliced tomato to the skillet and cook for an additional 1-2 minutes, just until heated through.
> Spread the cooked zucchini and tomato evenly across the bottom of the skillet.
> Pour the beaten eggs over the zucchini and tomato mixture in the skillet, making sure they are evenly distributed.
> Sprinkle the shredded cheese over the top of the frittata.
> Transfer the skillet to the preheated oven and bake for 15-20 minutes, or until the frittata is set in the center and lightly golden brown on top.
> Once cooked, remove the skillet from the oven and sprinkle the chopped fresh basil or parsley over the top of the frittata.
> Allow the frittata to cool for a few minutes before slicing it into wedges.
> Serve the zucchini and tomato frittata warm or at room temperature, garnished with additional fresh herbs if desired.

Enjoy your flavorful and nutritious zucchini and tomato frittata as a satisfying meal any time of day! It's great on its own or paired with a side salad or crusty bread.

Breakfast Stromboli

Ingredients:

- 1 pound pizza dough (store-bought or homemade)
- 6 large eggs
- 1/4 cup milk
- Salt and pepper to taste
- 1 cup shredded cheese (cheddar, mozzarella, or your choice)
- 6 slices of cooked bacon or ham, chopped
- 1/2 cup diced bell peppers (any color)
- 1/4 cup diced onions
- 1/4 cup chopped fresh parsley or chives (optional)
- Cooking spray or olive oil, for greasing
- Optional toppings: salsa, hot sauce, or sour cream

Instructions:

Preheat your oven to 375°F (190°C). Line a baking sheet with parchment paper or lightly grease it with cooking spray.
In a mixing bowl, whisk together the eggs, milk, salt, and pepper until well combined.
Heat a skillet over medium heat and add a little oil or butter. Pour the egg mixture into the skillet and scramble the eggs until they are just set. Remove from heat and set aside.
On a lightly floured surface, roll out the pizza dough into a rectangle, about 1/4 inch thick.
Sprinkle half of the shredded cheese evenly over the surface of the dough, leaving a border around the edges.
Spread the scrambled eggs evenly over the cheese layer, followed by the chopped bacon or ham, diced bell peppers, diced onions, and chopped parsley or chives, if using.
Sprinkle the remaining shredded cheese over the top of the filling.
Starting from one of the longer sides, carefully roll up the dough into a tight log, sealing the edges.
Transfer the rolled-up stromboli onto the prepared baking sheet, seam side down.
Using a sharp knife, make a few small slits in the top of the stromboli to allow steam to escape during baking.

Bake the stromboli in the preheated oven for 20-25 minutes, or until the crust is golden brown and crispy.

Remove the stromboli from the oven and let it cool for a few minutes before slicing it into thick slices.

Serve the breakfast stromboli warm, with optional toppings like salsa, hot sauce, or sour cream on the side.

Enjoy your delicious and hearty breakfast stromboli as a satisfying meal to start your day!

Breakfast Cobb Salad

Ingredients:

For the salad:

- 6 cups mixed salad greens (such as romaine, spinach, or arugula)
- 4 hard-boiled eggs, peeled and sliced
- 6 slices of bacon, cooked until crispy and chopped
- 1 cup cherry tomatoes, halved
- 1 avocado, diced
- 1/2 cup crumbled blue cheese or feta cheese
- 1/4 cup chopped green onions (optional)
- Salt and pepper to taste

For the dressing:

- 1/4 cup olive oil
- 2 tablespoons red wine vinegar
- 1 teaspoon Dijon mustard
- 1 teaspoon honey
- Salt and pepper to taste

Instructions:

In a large mixing bowl, combine the mixed salad greens, sliced hard-boiled eggs, chopped bacon, halved cherry tomatoes, diced avocado, crumbled blue cheese (or feta cheese), and chopped green onions (if using).
In a small jar with a lid, combine the olive oil, red wine vinegar, Dijon mustard, honey, salt, and pepper. Close the lid tightly and shake vigorously until the dressing is well combined.
Drizzle the dressing over the salad and toss gently to coat all the ingredients evenly.
Season the salad with additional salt and pepper to taste, if needed.
Divide the breakfast Cobb salad among serving plates or bowls.
Serve immediately and enjoy your delicious and nutritious breakfast Cobb salad!

Feel free to customize your breakfast Cobb salad with additional ingredients such as diced cooked chicken breast, sliced bell peppers, or crumbled cooked sausage. You can also swap out the dressing for your favorite vinaigrette or creamy dressing. It's a versatile dish that's perfect for breakfast or brunch!

Monte Cristo Sandwiches

Ingredients:

- 8 slices of sandwich bread (white or whole wheat)
- 8 slices of deli ham
- 8 slices of Swiss cheese
- 4 large eggs
- 1/2 cup milk
- 1/4 teaspoon salt
- 1/4 teaspoon black pepper
- 2 tablespoons unsalted butter
- Powdered sugar, for dusting
- Raspberry jam or maple syrup, for serving (optional)

Instructions:

Lay out four slices of bread on a clean surface. Top each slice with 2 slices of ham and 2 slices of Swiss cheese.
Place the remaining four slices of bread on top to form sandwiches.
In a shallow dish, whisk together the eggs, milk, salt, and pepper until well combined.
Heat a large skillet or griddle over medium heat. Add 1 tablespoon of butter and let it melt, spreading it evenly across the surface of the skillet.
Dip each sandwich into the egg mixture, making sure to coat both sides thoroughly.
Place the dipped sandwiches onto the preheated skillet or griddle. Cook for 3-4 minutes on each side, or until the sandwiches are golden brown and the cheese is melted.
Repeat with the remaining sandwiches, adding more butter to the skillet as needed.
Once cooked, remove the sandwiches from the skillet and transfer them to a cutting board.
Cut each sandwich diagonally into halves or quarters.
Dust the tops of the sandwiches with powdered sugar.
Serve the Monte Cristo sandwiches warm, with raspberry jam or maple syrup on the side for dipping, if desired.

Enjoy your delicious Monte Cristo sandwiches as a delightful brunch or lunch option! They're perfect for special occasions or whenever you're craving a sweet and savory treat.

Veggie Breakfast Burritos

Ingredients:

- 6 large eggs
- 1 tablespoon olive oil
- 1 bell pepper, diced
- 1 small onion, diced
- 1 cup diced tomatoes
- 1 cup cooked black beans (canned or homemade)
- 1 cup diced cooked potatoes (such as hash browns or roasted potatoes)
- 1 cup shredded cheese (cheddar, Monterey Jack, or a Mexican cheese blend)
- 6 large flour tortillas
- Salt and pepper to taste
- Optional toppings: salsa, avocado slices, sour cream, chopped cilantro

Instructions:

In a large skillet, heat the olive oil over medium heat. Add the diced bell pepper and onion to the skillet and sauté until they are softened, about 5 minutes.
While the bell pepper and onion are cooking, crack the eggs into a mixing bowl and whisk them together. Season with salt and pepper to taste.
Push the cooked bell pepper and onion to one side of the skillet, and pour the beaten eggs into the other side. Scramble the eggs until they are cooked through.
Once the eggs are cooked, stir them together with the bell pepper and onion mixture in the skillet.
Add the diced tomatoes, cooked black beans, and cooked potatoes to the skillet. Stir everything together and cook for an additional 2-3 minutes, until heated through.
Sprinkle the shredded cheese evenly over the filling mixture in the skillet. Let it melt slightly.
Warm the flour tortillas in a microwave or skillet for a few seconds to make them pliable.
Spoon a portion of the veggie and egg filling onto each tortilla, slightly off-center.
Fold the sides of the tortilla over the filling, then roll it up tightly from the bottom to enclose the filling completely.
Repeat with the remaining tortillas and filling mixture to make 6 veggie breakfast burritos.

Serve the veggie breakfast burritos warm, with optional toppings such as salsa, avocado slices, sour cream, or chopped cilantro.

Enjoy your delicious and nutritious veggie breakfast burritos for a satisfying morning meal! They're perfect for meal prep or on-the-go breakfasts.

Breakfast Stuffed Peppers

Ingredients:

- 4 large bell peppers (any color), halved and seeds removed
- 8 large eggs
- 1 cup cooked breakfast sausage or bacon, diced
- 1 cup shredded cheddar cheese
- 1/2 cup diced onion
- 1/2 cup diced tomatoes
- Salt and pepper to taste
- Optional: chopped fresh herbs like parsley or chives for garnish

Instructions:

Preheat your oven to 375°F (190°C). Line a baking sheet with parchment paper or lightly grease it.
Place the halved bell peppers cut-side up on the prepared baking sheet.
In a large mixing bowl, whisk together the eggs until well beaten. Season with salt and pepper to taste.
Stir in the cooked breakfast sausage or bacon, shredded cheddar cheese, diced onion, and diced tomatoes into the beaten eggs until well combined.
Spoon the egg mixture evenly into each bell pepper half, filling them to the top.
Bake in the preheated oven for about 25-30 minutes or until the eggs are set and the peppers are tender.
Once cooked, remove the stuffed peppers from the oven and let them cool for a few minutes before serving.
Garnish with chopped fresh herbs if desired and serve hot.

These breakfast stuffed peppers are not only flavorful but also customizable. You can add other ingredients like spinach, mushrooms, or different types of cheese according to your preference. Enjoy your delicious and nutritious breakfast!

Hash Brown Casserole

Ingredients:

- 1 (30 oz) package frozen shredded hash browns, thawed
- 1/2 cup unsalted butter, melted
- 1 (10.5 oz) can condensed cream of chicken soup
- 1 (8 oz) container sour cream
- 1 small onion, finely chopped
- 2 cups shredded cheddar cheese
- 1 teaspoon garlic powder
- 1/2 teaspoon salt
- 1/4 teaspoon black pepper
- 2 cups crushed cornflakes
- 1/4 cup unsalted butter, melted

Instructions:

Preheat your oven to 350°F (175°C). Grease a 9x13-inch baking dish.
In a large mixing bowl, combine the thawed hash browns, melted butter, condensed cream of chicken soup, sour cream, chopped onion, shredded cheddar cheese, garlic powder, salt, and black pepper. Mix well until all ingredients are evenly combined.
Spread the hash brown mixture evenly into the prepared baking dish.
In a separate bowl, mix together the crushed cornflakes and melted butter until well combined.
Sprinkle the buttered cornflake mixture evenly over the top of the hash brown mixture in the baking dish.
Cover the baking dish with aluminum foil and bake in the preheated oven for 45 minutes.
After 45 minutes, remove the foil and continue baking for an additional 15 minutes or until the casserole is hot and bubbly, and the top is golden brown.
Once cooked, remove the casserole from the oven and let it cool for a few minutes before serving.
Serve warm and enjoy your delicious hash brown casserole!

This casserole is a crowd-pleaser and can be easily customized by adding ingredients like cooked bacon, diced ham, or chopped bell peppers according to your taste preferences. It's a perfect dish for a leisurely weekend breakfast or brunch with family and friends.

Brioche French Toast

Ingredients:

- 1 loaf of brioche bread, preferably a day or two old, sliced into thick slices
- 4 large eggs
- 1 cup milk
- 1 teaspoon vanilla extract
- 1/2 teaspoon ground cinnamon
- Pinch of salt
- Butter or cooking spray for greasing the skillet
- Maple syrup, fresh berries, powdered sugar, or other toppings of your choice for serving

Instructions:

In a shallow dish or pie plate, whisk together the eggs, milk, vanilla extract, ground cinnamon, and a pinch of salt until well combined.

Heat a large skillet or griddle over medium heat. Add a small amount of butter or coat with cooking spray to prevent sticking.

Dip each slice of brioche bread into the egg mixture, ensuring both sides are well coated but not overly saturated.

Place the dipped slices of brioche onto the preheated skillet or griddle. Cook until golden brown on one side, about 2-3 minutes.

Flip the slices of brioche and cook until golden brown on the other side, another 2-3 minutes.

Remove the French toast from the skillet and transfer to a plate. Repeat with the remaining slices of brioche, adding more butter or cooking spray to the skillet as needed.

Serve the brioche French toast warm with maple syrup, fresh berries, powdered sugar, or any other toppings you prefer.

Enjoy your delicious and decadent brioche French toast! It's perfect for a leisurely weekend breakfast or brunch with loved ones.

Chicken and Waffle Sliders

Ingredients:

- 1 pound boneless, skinless chicken breasts, cut into small slider-sized pieces
- 1 cup all-purpose flour
- 1 teaspoon salt
- 1/2 teaspoon black pepper
- 1/2 teaspoon paprika
- 1/2 teaspoon garlic powder
- 2 large eggs
- 1/4 cup milk
- 2 cups breadcrumbs (you can use plain or seasoned breadcrumbs)
- Vegetable oil for frying
- Mini waffles (store-bought or homemade)
- Maple syrup, for serving
- Optional toppings: lettuce, tomato slices, pickles, mayonnaise, hot sauce, etc.

Instructions:

In a shallow dish, mix together the all-purpose flour, salt, black pepper, paprika, and garlic powder.
In another shallow dish, whisk together the eggs and milk to create an egg wash.
Place the breadcrumbs in a third shallow dish.
Dredge each piece of chicken in the flour mixture, shaking off any excess.
Dip the floured chicken pieces into the egg wash, allowing any excess to drip off.
Coat the chicken pieces evenly with breadcrumbs, pressing gently to adhere.
Heat vegetable oil in a large skillet over medium-high heat until it reaches 350°F (175°C).
Carefully place the breaded chicken pieces into the hot oil in batches, making sure not to overcrowd the skillet. Fry until golden brown and cooked through, about 4-5 minutes per side. Transfer the cooked chicken to a paper towel-lined plate to drain any excess oil.
Meanwhile, toast the mini waffles according to the package instructions or until they are crisp and golden brown.
To assemble the sliders, place a piece of fried chicken on top of a mini waffle. Drizzle with maple syrup and add any desired toppings, such as lettuce, tomato slices, pickles, mayonnaise, or hot sauce.
Top with another mini waffle to form a sandwich.
Repeat with the remaining chicken and waffles to make additional sliders.

Serve the chicken and waffle sliders warm and enjoy!

These sliders make a fantastic appetizer, brunch dish, or even a fun dinner option.

They're sure to be a hit at any gathering!

Breakfast Empanadas

Ingredients:

For the Dough:

- 2 cups all-purpose flour
- 1/2 teaspoon salt
- 1/2 cup cold unsalted butter, cut into small cubes
- 1/4 cup cold water
- 1 egg (for egg wash)

For the Filling:

- 6 large eggs
- 1/2 cup cooked breakfast sausage, crumbled
- 1/2 cup cooked bacon, chopped
- 1/2 cup shredded cheddar cheese
- 1/4 cup chopped green onions or chives
- Salt and pepper to taste

Instructions:

1. Prepare the Dough:

   In a large mixing bowl, whisk together the flour and salt.
   Add the cold cubed butter to the flour mixture. Use a pastry cutter or fork to cut the butter into the flour until the mixture resembles coarse crumbs.
   Gradually add the cold water, a little at a time, mixing until the dough comes together. Be careful not to overwork the dough.
   Shape the dough into a ball, wrap it in plastic wrap, and refrigerate for at least 30 minutes to chill.

2. Prepare the Filling:

   In a skillet over medium heat, scramble the eggs until just cooked through. Season with salt and pepper to taste. Remove from heat.
   In a large mixing bowl, combine the scrambled eggs, crumbled breakfast sausage, chopped bacon, shredded cheddar cheese, and chopped green onions or chives. Mix well to combine.

3. Assemble the Empanadas:

Preheat your oven to 375°F (190°C). Line a baking sheet with parchment paper.

On a lightly floured surface, roll out the chilled dough to about 1/8 inch thickness.

Use a round cutter (about 4-5 inches in diameter) to cut out circles from the dough.

Place a spoonful of the breakfast filling onto one half of each dough circle, leaving a small border around the edges.

Fold the other half of the dough circle over the filling to create a half-moon shape. Press the edges firmly to seal.

Use a fork to crimp the edges of the empanadas, or you can twist and fold the edges to create a decorative pattern.

Place the assembled empanadas onto the prepared baking sheet.

In a small bowl, beat the egg for the egg wash. Brush the tops of the empanadas with the egg wash.

Bake in the preheated oven for 20-25 minutes or until the empanadas are golden brown and crispy.

4. Serve:

Allow the breakfast empanadas to cool for a few minutes before serving.

Enjoy them warm on their own or with your favorite breakfast condiments, such as salsa, hot sauce, or sour cream.

These breakfast empanadas are perfect for meal prep or on-the-go breakfasts. They can be stored in the refrigerator and reheated in the oven or microwave for a quick and satisfying morning meal.

Spinach and Bacon Quiche

Ingredients:

For the Crust:

- 1 1/4 cups all-purpose flour
- 1/2 teaspoon salt
- 1/2 cup cold unsalted butter, cut into small cubes
- 3-4 tablespoons ice water

For the Filling:

- 6 slices bacon, cooked and crumbled
- 2 cups fresh baby spinach, roughly chopped
- 1 cup shredded Swiss cheese (or any cheese of your choice)
- 4 large eggs
- 1 cup heavy cream (or half-and-half)
- 1/2 teaspoon salt
- 1/4 teaspoon black pepper
- 1/4 teaspoon ground nutmeg (optional)

Instructions:

1. Prepare the Crust:

    In a food processor, combine the all-purpose flour and salt. Pulse a few times to mix.
    Add the cold cubed butter to the flour mixture. Pulse until the mixture resembles coarse crumbs.
    With the food processor running, gradually add the ice water, one tablespoon at a time, until the dough comes together and forms a ball.
    Turn the dough out onto a lightly floured surface. Shape it into a disk, wrap it in plastic wrap, and refrigerate for at least 30 minutes to chill.

2. Preheat the Oven:

    - Preheat your oven to 375°F (190°C).

3. Roll out the Crust:

On a lightly floured surface, roll out the chilled dough into a circle about 12 inches in diameter.

Transfer the rolled-out dough to a 9-inch pie dish. Press it gently into the bottom and sides of the dish. Trim any excess dough hanging over the edges.

4. Prepare the Filling:

In a skillet over medium heat, cook the bacon until crispy. Remove the bacon from the skillet and drain on paper towels. Crumble the bacon into small pieces.

In the same skillet with the bacon fat, add the chopped spinach. Cook until wilted, about 2-3 minutes. Remove from heat and set aside.

In a mixing bowl, whisk together the eggs, heavy cream, salt, black pepper, and ground nutmeg (if using) until well combined.

5. Assemble the Quiche:

Sprinkle the crumbled bacon and cooked spinach evenly over the bottom of the prepared pie crust.

Sprinkle the shredded Swiss cheese over the bacon and spinach.

Pour the egg mixture over the filling ingredients in the pie crust.

6. Bake:

Place the quiche in the preheated oven and bake for 35-40 minutes or until the filling is set and the top is golden brown.

If the edges of the crust start to brown too quickly, you can cover them with aluminum foil or a pie crust shield halfway through baking.

Once baked, remove the quiche from the oven and let it cool for a few minutes before slicing.

7. Serve:

- Serve slices of the spinach and bacon quiche warm or at room temperature. Enjoy!

This quiche can be served as a main dish for brunch, lunch, or dinner, and it pairs well with a simple green salad or fresh fruit on the side. leftovers can be stored in the refrigerator for a few days and reheated in the oven or microwave.

Caramelized Onion and Gruyere Quiche

Ingredients:

For the Crust:

- 1 1/4 cups all-purpose flour
- 1/2 teaspoon salt
- 1/2 cup cold unsalted butter, cut into small cubes
- 3-4 tablespoons ice water

For the Filling:

- 2 large onions, thinly sliced
- 2 tablespoons unsalted butter
- 1 tablespoon olive oil
- Salt and pepper to taste
- 1 cup shredded Gruyere cheese
- 4 large eggs
- 1 cup heavy cream (or half-and-half)
- 1/2 teaspoon salt
- 1/4 teaspoon black pepper
- Pinch of nutmeg (optional)

Instructions:

1. Prepare the Crust:

   In a food processor, combine the all-purpose flour and salt. Pulse a few times to mix.
   Add the cold cubed butter to the flour mixture. Pulse until the mixture resembles coarse crumbs.
   With the food processor running, gradually add the ice water, one tablespoon at a time, until the dough comes together and forms a ball.
   Turn the dough out onto a lightly floured surface. Shape it into a disk, wrap it in plastic wrap, and refrigerate for at least 30 minutes to chill.

2. Caramelize the Onions:

   In a large skillet, heat the butter and olive oil over medium-low heat. Add the thinly sliced onions and cook, stirring occasionally, until they are caramelized and golden brown, about 25-30 minutes. Season with salt and pepper to taste. Remove from heat and let cool slightly.

3. Preheat the Oven:

- Preheat your oven to 375°F (190°C).

4. Roll out the Crust:

On a lightly floured surface, roll out the chilled dough into a circle about 12 inches in diameter.
Transfer the rolled-out dough to a 9-inch pie dish. Press it gently into the bottom and sides of the dish. Trim any excess dough hanging over the edges.

5. Prepare the Filling:

Spread the caramelized onions evenly over the bottom of the prepared pie crust.
Sprinkle the shredded Gruyere cheese over the caramelized onions.

6. Prepare the Custard:

In a mixing bowl, whisk together the eggs, heavy cream, salt, black pepper, and pinch of nutmeg (if using) until well combined.

7. Assemble the Quiche:

Pour the egg mixture over the caramelized onions and cheese in the pie crust.

8. Bake:

Place the quiche in the preheated oven and bake for 35-40 minutes or until the filling is set and the top is golden brown.
If the edges of the crust start to brown too quickly, you can cover them with aluminum foil or a pie crust shield halfway through baking.

9. Serve:

- Serve slices of the caramelized onion and Gruyere quiche warm or at room temperature. Enjoy!

This quiche is perfect for brunch, lunch, or a light dinner. Pair it with a simple green salad or roasted vegetables for a complete meal. leftovers can be stored in the refrigerator for a few days and reheated in the oven or microwave.

Breakfast Bruschetta

Ingredients:

- 4 slices of crusty bread (baguette or Italian bread works well)
- 4 large eggs
- 1 ripe avocado, mashed
- 1 cup cherry tomatoes, halved
- 1/4 cup diced red onion
- 1 tablespoon chopped fresh parsley or basil
- 1 tablespoon olive oil
- Salt and pepper to taste
- Optional: crumbled bacon, shredded cheese, hot sauce, or other toppings of your choice

Instructions:

Preheat your oven to 375°F (190°C). Place the bread slices on a baking sheet and toast them in the oven until lightly golden brown, about 5-7 minutes.

While the bread is toasting, prepare the toppings. In a small bowl, mix together the halved cherry tomatoes, diced red onion, chopped parsley or basil, and olive oil. Season with salt and pepper to taste. Set aside.

In a skillet over medium heat, fry or scramble the eggs according to your preference. Season with salt and pepper to taste.

Once the bread slices are toasted, remove them from the oven and spread the mashed avocado evenly over each slice.

Top the avocado-covered bread slices with the cooked eggs, dividing them equally among the slices.

Spoon the tomato and onion mixture over the eggs on each slice of bread.

If desired, add additional toppings such as crumbled bacon, shredded cheese, or hot sauce.

Serve the breakfast bruschetta immediately, while the bread is still warm.

Enjoy your delicious and flavorful breakfast bruschetta!

This breakfast bruschetta is versatile, and you can customize it with your favorite ingredients. It's a great way to start your day with a satisfying and nutritious meal.

Breakfast Enchiladas

Ingredients:

For the Enchilada Sauce:

- 2 tablespoons vegetable oil
- 2 tablespoons all-purpose flour
- 2 tablespoons chili powder
- 1 teaspoon ground cumin
- 1/2 teaspoon garlic powder
- 1/4 teaspoon dried oregano
- 1/4 teaspoon salt
- 1/4 teaspoon black pepper
- 2 cups chicken or vegetable broth

For the Enchiladas:

- 8 small flour tortillas
- 6 large eggs, scrambled
- 1 cup cooked breakfast sausage or bacon, crumbled
- 1 cup shredded cheddar cheese
- 1/2 cup diced bell peppers
- 1/2 cup diced onions
- Salt and pepper to taste
- Chopped fresh cilantro, for garnish
- Optional toppings: sliced avocado, sour cream, salsa, hot sauce, etc.

Instructions:

1. Prepare the Enchilada Sauce:

   In a saucepan, heat the vegetable oil over medium heat.
   Add the flour, chili powder, cumin, garlic powder, oregano, salt, and black pepper.
   Cook, stirring constantly, for about 1 minute to toast the spices.
   Gradually whisk in the chicken or vegetable broth, ensuring there are no lumps.
   Bring the mixture to a simmer and cook for 5-7 minutes, stirring occasionally, until the sauce has thickened. Remove from heat and set aside.

2. Prepare the Enchiladas:

Preheat your oven to 375°F (190°C). Grease a 9x13-inch baking dish.

In a skillet over medium heat, scramble the eggs until just cooked through. Season with salt and pepper to taste. Remove from heat.

In a large mixing bowl, combine the scrambled eggs, cooked breakfast sausage or bacon, shredded cheddar cheese, diced bell peppers, and diced onions. Mix well to combine.

3. Assemble the Enchiladas:

   Pour a small amount of the prepared enchilada sauce into the bottom of the greased baking dish, spreading it evenly.

   Spoon the egg and sausage mixture onto each flour tortilla, dividing it evenly among them. Roll up the tortillas and place them seam-side down in the baking dish.

4. Bake:

   Pour the remaining enchilada sauce over the assembled enchiladas, spreading it evenly to cover them.

   Sprinkle additional shredded cheese on top if desired.

   Cover the baking dish with aluminum foil and bake in the preheated oven for 20-25 minutes, or until the enchiladas are heated through and the cheese is melted and bubbly.

5. Serve:

   Remove the foil from the baking dish and garnish the enchiladas with chopped fresh cilantro.

   Serve the breakfast enchiladas hot with your favorite toppings such as sliced avocado, sour cream, salsa, or hot sauce.

Enjoy your delicious and satisfying breakfast enchiladas! They're perfect for a weekend brunch or any morning when you want to start your day with a flavorful meal.

Breakfast Nachos

Ingredients:

- 1 bag of tortilla chips
- 6 large eggs
- 1 cup cooked breakfast sausage or bacon, crumbled
- 1 cup shredded cheddar cheese
- 1 cup diced bell peppers
- 1/2 cup diced onions
- 1/2 cup diced tomatoes
- 1/4 cup sliced black olives
- 1/4 cup sliced jalapeños (optional)
- Salt and pepper to taste
- Fresh cilantro, chopped, for garnish
- Sour cream, salsa, and guacamole for serving

Instructions:

Preheat your oven to 375°F (190°C). Line a baking sheet with parchment paper.
Spread the tortilla chips in a single layer on the prepared baking sheet.
In a skillet over medium heat, scramble the eggs until just cooked through.
Season with salt and pepper to taste.
Evenly distribute the scrambled eggs over the tortilla chips.
Sprinkle the cooked breakfast sausage or bacon, shredded cheddar cheese, diced bell peppers, diced onions, diced tomatoes, sliced black olives, and sliced jalapeños (if using) over the scrambled eggs and tortilla chips.
Place the baking sheet in the preheated oven and bake for 10-12 minutes, or until the cheese is melted and bubbly.
Remove the baking sheet from the oven and let the breakfast nachos cool for a few minutes.
Garnish the breakfast nachos with chopped fresh cilantro.
Serve the breakfast nachos hot with sour cream, salsa, and guacamole on the side for dipping.

Enjoy your delicious and customizable breakfast nachos! They're perfect for a weekend brunch or whenever you're craving a savory breakfast treat.

Bacon and Cheddar Scones

Ingredients:

- 2 cups all-purpose flour
- 1 tablespoon baking powder
- 1/2 teaspoon baking soda
- 1/2 teaspoon salt
- 1/2 cup cold unsalted butter, cut into small cubes
- 1/2 cup cooked bacon, chopped
- 1 cup shredded cheddar cheese
- 1/4 cup chopped chives or green onions
- 3/4 cup buttermilk
- 1 large egg
- 1 tablespoon honey (optional, for a touch of sweetness)

Instructions:

Preheat your oven to 400°F (200°C). Line a baking sheet with parchment paper.
In a large mixing bowl, whisk together the flour, baking powder, baking soda, and salt.
Add the cold cubed butter to the flour mixture. Use a pastry cutter or fork to cut the butter into the flour until the mixture resembles coarse crumbs.
Stir in the chopped bacon, shredded cheddar cheese, and chopped chives or green onions until evenly distributed.
In a separate bowl, whisk together the buttermilk, egg, and honey (if using) until well combined.
Pour the buttermilk mixture into the flour mixture. Use a spatula or wooden spoon to gently stir until the dough comes together. Be careful not to overmix.
Turn the dough out onto a lightly floured surface. Pat it into a circle about 1 inch thick.
Use a sharp knife or a pastry cutter to cut the dough into 8 wedges.
Place the wedges onto the prepared baking sheet, leaving space between each scone.
Optional: Brush the tops of the scones with a little extra buttermilk or beaten egg for a golden finish.
Bake in the preheated oven for 15-18 minutes, or until the scones are golden brown and cooked through.
Remove the scones from the oven and let them cool on the baking sheet for a few minutes before transferring them to a wire rack to cool completely.

Enjoy your delicious bacon and cheddar scones warm or at room temperature. They're perfect served with a pat of butter or a dollop of your favorite spread.

Ham and Cheese Croissants

Ingredients:

- 1 sheet of puff pastry, thawed (you can use store-bought or homemade)
- 4 slices of ham
- 4 slices of cheese (such as Swiss or Gruyere)
- 1 egg, beaten (for egg wash)
- Sesame seeds or poppy seeds for topping (optional)

Instructions:

Preheat your oven to 400°F (200°C). Line a baking sheet with parchment paper.
Roll out the puff pastry sheet on a lightly floured surface into a large rectangle, about 1/4 inch thick.
Using a sharp knife or pizza cutter, cut the rectangle into 4 smaller rectangles.
Place a slice of ham and a slice of cheese on each rectangle of puff pastry.
Roll up each rectangle from the shorter side, enclosing the ham and cheese inside. Place the seam side down on the prepared baking sheet.
Repeat with the remaining rectangles of puff pastry, ham, and cheese.
Brush the tops of the croissants with the beaten egg to create a shiny finish.
If desired, sprinkle sesame seeds or poppy seeds over the tops of the croissants for added flavor and texture.
Bake in the preheated oven for 15-20 minutes, or until the croissants are golden brown and puffed up.
Remove from the oven and let the croissants cool slightly before serving.

Enjoy your delicious ham and cheese croissants warm from the oven. They're perfect for a leisurely breakfast or brunch, and they also make a great grab-and-go option for busy mornings.

Breakfast Strata with Sausage and Peppers

Ingredients:

- 1 pound Italian sausage, casings removed
- 1 red bell pepper, diced
- 1 green bell pepper, diced
- 1 small onion, diced
- 8 cups bread cubes (such as French bread or sourdough), cut into 1-inch cubes
- 2 cups shredded cheddar cheese
- 8 large eggs
- 2 cups milk
- 1 teaspoon Dijon mustard
- 1/2 teaspoon salt
- 1/4 teaspoon black pepper
- 1/4 teaspoon paprika
- 1/4 teaspoon dried thyme
- 1/4 teaspoon dried oregano
- 1/4 teaspoon dried basil
- Chopped fresh parsley for garnish

Instructions:

Preheat your oven to 350°F (175°C). Grease a 9x13-inch baking dish.

In a skillet over medium heat, cook the Italian sausage, breaking it apart with a spoon, until browned and cooked through. Remove the cooked sausage from the skillet and set aside.

In the same skillet, add the diced bell peppers and onion. Cook until softened, about 5-7 minutes. Remove from heat and set aside.

In the prepared baking dish, layer half of the bread cubes, cooked sausage, cooked peppers and onions, and shredded cheddar cheese. Repeat with the remaining ingredients, ending with a layer of cheese on top.

In a large mixing bowl, whisk together the eggs, milk, Dijon mustard, salt, black pepper, paprika, dried thyme, dried oregano, and dried basil until well combined.

Pour the egg mixture evenly over the layered ingredients in the baking dish, pressing down gently to ensure the bread is soaked in the egg mixture.

Cover the baking dish with aluminum foil and let it sit in the refrigerator for at least 1 hour, or overnight if preparing ahead.

When ready to bake, remove the baking dish from the refrigerator and let it sit at room temperature while the oven preheats.

Bake the strata, covered with foil, in the preheated oven for 45 minutes. Then, remove the foil and bake for an additional 15-20 minutes, or until the top is golden brown and the eggs are set.
Remove from the oven and let the strata cool for a few minutes before slicing. Garnish with chopped fresh parsley before serving.

Enjoy your delicious breakfast strata with sausage and peppers! It's perfect for a weekend brunch or any special occasion breakfast.

www.ingramcontent.com/pod-product-compliance
Lightning Source LLC
LaVergne TN
LVHW061946070526
838199LV00060B/3998